BELUGA WHALES

A TRUE BOOK®

by
Ann O. Squire

Children's Press®

A Division of Scholastic Inc.

New York Toronto London Auckland Sydney
Mexico City New Delhi Hong Kong
Danbury, Connecticut

A beluga whale with trainer at the Vancouver Aquarium

Content Consultant
Kathy Carlstead, PhD
Research Scientist
Honolulu Zoo

Reading Consultant
Cecilia Minden-Cupp, PhD
Former Director, Language and
Literacy Program
Harvard Graduate School of
Education

Author's Dedication
For Emma

The photograph on the cover shows a beluga whale at the Vancouver Aquarium in Canada. The photograph on the title pages shows a group of adult beluga whales surfacing.

Library of Congress Cataloging-in-Publication Data
Squire, Ann.
    Beluga whales / by Ann O. Squire.
        p. cm. — (A True Book)
    Includes bibliographical references and index.
    ISBN-10: 0-516-25469-3 (lib. bdg)   0-516-25580-0 (pbk.)
    ISBN-13: 978-0-516-25469-2 (lib. bdg.) 978-0-516-25580-4 (pbk.)
    1. White whale—Juvenile literature. I. Title. II. Series.
QL737.C433S69 2006
599.5'42—dc22   2005003272

CHILDREN'S PRESS, and A TRUE BOOK™, and associated logos are trademarks and/or registered trademarks of Scholastic Library Publishing. SCHOLASTIC and associated logos are trademarks and/or registered trademarks of Scholastic Inc.
2 3 4 5 6 7 8 9 10 R 16 15 14 13 12 11 10 09 08 07   62

Contents

A killer whale hunts in the ocean.

Little White Whales

What do you think of when you hear the word *whale*? Do you imagine a gigantic blue whale breaking the water's surface and diving back into the deep ocean? Or do you think of a fierce black and white killer whale chasing its dinner?

These two kinds of whales might be the most familiar, but they are not the only whales in the ocean. In fact, there are about eighty kinds of whales living in Earth's waters today.

One of the most interesting whales is the beluga. The beluga is a pure-white whale that lives in the icy waters of the Arctic and nearby seas. Some belugas live in rivers in Canada.

A beluga, also called the white whale, spouts at the water's surface.

The beluga (below) is much smaller than the blue whale (left).

For a whale, the beluga is small. It grows to be only about 15 feet (4.6 meters) long. A blue whale, in contrast, can reach nearly 100 feet (31 m) long. That's about three times as long as a school bus.

Belugas have smooth, sleek bodies that help them move easily through the water. They also have a thick layer of fat called **blubber** to protect them against the cold.

Blubber makes up more than 40 percent of a beluga's body weight. That means that an adult beluga weighing 3,000 pounds (1,362 kilograms) carries more than 1,200 pounds (545 kg) of fat!

Belugas belong to a group of mostly ocean animals called **Cetacea**. This group includes all whales and dolphins. Every member of this group is either a baleen whale or a toothed whale.

Fat called blubber helps keep the beluga whale warm in the Arctic water.

Baleen whales use filters called baleen to feed (top). Toothed whales eat with their teeth (bottom).

Blue whales and sperm whales are baleen whales. They do not have teeth. They feed by sucking in seawater and straining out tiny bits of food through huge filters in the mouth called **baleen**.

Beluga whales are toothed whales. Killer whales, narwhals, porpoises, and dolphins are also toothed whales. Belugas and other toothed whales hunt for their food. They eat fish, squid, octopus, and shellfish.

Life in the Pod

Belugas like to be together. They live in groups called **pods**. A pod can have as many as twenty-five whales. The leader of the pod is usually a large male. The other pod members are smaller males and females without young. Mothers and their young often make up their own pods.

Belugas live and travel in groups called pods.

Many different pods may travel together in herds. It was once common to see herds of several thousand belugas swimming south to warmer waters in the fall, or returning north several months later.

Belugas hunt together, too. They surround schools of fish. Then the belugas drive the fish into shallow water and eat them whole.

Belugas also hunt on their own, looking for shellfish and

This view from the sky shows a herd of beluga whales in Canada's Northwest Territories.

A flexible neck helps the beluga whale search for food.

worms along the sea bottom.
Unlike most other whales and

18

dolphins, the beluga can move its neck easily. It turns its head from side to side to search for food.

Belugas communicate well with each other. They touch each other and make expressions with their faces. They also make many sounds, which range from squeaks and whistles to clucks and moos. Belugas make so much noise that they have been called "canaries of the sea."

A Beluga's Body

Although belugas and other whales live in the ocean, they are **mammals** just like us. They are warm-blooded animals that nurse their young. They also breathe air.

Of course, whales and humans don't breathe in the same way. We breathe through our noses.

A beluga whale breathes through its blowhole.

A whale uses a **blowhole**. The blowhole is a nostril on top of the beluga's head.

When the beluga goes underwater,
a flap closes over its blowhole.

When the beluga whale dives underwater, a flap closes over the blowhole to keep water out. When the beluga whale heads back up, it opens the blowhole just before it reaches the surface. It also blows out the breath it was holding under-water. This distinctive spout is what whale watchers and hunters look for when they are trying to spot whales.

After exhaling, the beluga quickly takes another breath of

A beluga whale holds its breath underwater.

air before diving again. It can hold its breath underwater for as long as twenty minutes.

An Unusual Ridge

Belugas at an ice hole

A dorsal fin is the triangle-shaped fin on the back of most toothed whales. The beluga whale does not have one of these fins. Scientists believe a dorsal fin would make it difficult for the beluga to swim underneath the thick Arctic ice. The beluga does have a hardened ridge along its back. When the whale needs to come up for air, this ridge helps break through ice up to 4 inches (10 centimeters) thick!

A beluga whale shows his flippers at Chicago's Shedd Aquarium.

The beluga's body is like ours in other ways as well. If you could see the bones of a beluga's front flippers, you would see that they look much like a human's hand. Our hands are made for grasping and holding things. The beluga's flippers help steer the animal through the water.

We already learned that belugas "talk" to each other. Belugas also use sound to find food when it is hard to see in the water.

The beluga makes clicking sounds. These sounds pass through the **melon**. The melon is a fatty organ in the whale's forehead. The melon focuses the clicks into a beam of sound. This beam of sound bounces off objects and comes back to the whale as an echo.

Belugas can tell a lot from these echoes. They can tell how far away something is, how big it is, and what shape

On the beluga's forehead is a fatty organ called the melon.

it is. Finding objects by sending out pulses of sound and listening for their echoes is called **echolocation**.

Although the beluga has ears, it hears most sounds through its lower jawbone.

It is probably no surprise that the beluga has excellent hearing. Its ears are tiny openings just behind the eyes. But the beluga actually hears most sounds through its jawbone.

The lower jawbone is hollow and filled with fat. Sound waves seem to pass through the fat-filled jawbone to the bones of the middle ear. They in turn send signals to the whale's brain.

Beluga Babies

Beluga whales mate in early spring. A female beluga is ready to mate when she is about five years old. She mates every two or three years. The male beluga is usually ready to mate when he is about eight years old.

After more than a year, the pregnant female is ready to give

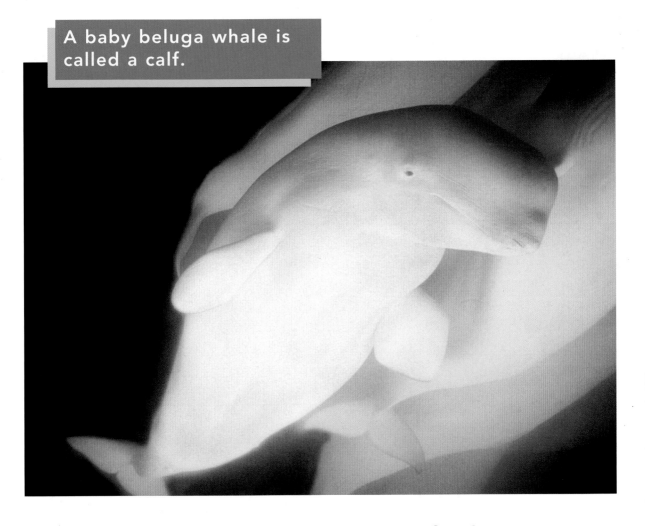

A baby beluga whale is called a calf.

birth to her baby, or **calf**. She will have the calf in a bay or river. The water is warmer there than in the open ocean.

A gray baby beluga swims close to its mother.

The female beluga may be surrounded by other whales as she gives birth. They may press against her, helping to deliver the calf safely.

A baby beluga measures about 5 feet (1.5 m) long. It weighs 175 pounds (79 kg). The calf is not white, like its parents, but a dark brownish-gray. The calf's color will fade to light gray over time.

When a beluga whale is white, that means it has grown into an adult. Scientists can estimate a beluga's age by examining its color. The lighter the beluga, the older it is.

A baby beluga can swim at birth. But it needs its mother's help to reach the surface for its first breath of air.

The calf depends entirely on its mother for food. The baby beluga will live off its mother's milk until its teeth grow in, after about one year. Some beluga babies drink mother's milk even after they are able to find their own food.

The calf learns how to hunt by watching its mother and

Beluga mothers travel with their calves in a pod.

the other adults in the pod. It takes two years for the beluga baby to learn. Now it is ready to survive on its own.

Threats to Belugas

Belugas in the open sea face many dangers. Belugas swim slowly, so killer whales sometimes attack them. Polar bears waiting on large chunks of ice can capture belugas when they come to the surface for air. But most belugas killed in the wild are not killed by

A polar bear prepares to attack a beluga whale trapped in an ice hole.

whales or polar bears. Most are killed by humans and their activities.

As part of their traditions, these Arctic people cut and dry their beluga catch.

For years and years, people of the Arctic have hunted belugas for their hide, meat, and oil. Even so, hunting is not the biggest threat to belugas.

Today, in Canada's Saint Lawrence River, the main dangers to belugas come from water pollution. Factories dump dangerous chemicals into the water. These chemicals increase the belugas' chances of developing deadly diseases. Chemical pollution can also reduce the number of healthy calves that are born.

Some organizations are fighting for laws to keep Arctic waters clean for the animals that live there, including the belugas. Aquariums around the world are studying belugas to learn more about how they live, feed, and mate.

If you are interested in beluga whales, you might like to visit an aquarium. You could learn more about these amazing mammals and see one up close. If enough people are informed about beluga whales and about the importance of keeping the oceans and rivers

A young visitor observes a beluga whale at the Vancouver Aquarium.

clean for them, these little white whales will be with us for many years to come.

To Find Out More

Here are some additional resources to help you learn more about beluga whales:

 **Books**

Gunzi, Christiane. **The Best Book of Whales and Dolphins**. Kingfisher, 2001.

Hirschmann, Kris. **Beluga Whales**. KidHaven Press, 2004.

Martin, Tony. **Beluga Whales**. Voyageur Press, 1996.

Paine, Stefani. **The World of the Arctic Whales: Belugas, Bowheads, and Narwhals**. Sierra Club Books for Children, 1995.

Pringle, Laurence P., and Meryl Henderson (illustrator). **Whales! Strange and Wonderful**. Boyds Mills Press, 2003.

Skerry, Brian. **A Whale on Her Own: The True Story of Wilma the Beluga Whale**. Blackbirch Press, 2002.

Organizations and Online Sites

The Ocean Conservancy
2029 K Street
Washington, DC 20006
800-519-1541
*http://www.ocean
conservancy.org/*

Learn more about the Ocean Conservancy and its various programs. Click on "Fish and Wildlife" to link to a page about beluga whales.

Whale and Dolphin Conservation Society
Brookfield House
38 Saint Paul Street
Chippenham, Wiltshire
SN15 1LY
United Kingdom
http://www.wdcs.org

This organization is dedicated to the protection of whales, dolphins, and their environment. Its site has fascinating facts about beluga whales, whale-related games and activities, and the latest news about beluga whales around the world.

OceanLink
*http://oceanlink.island.net/
oinfo/acoustics/ListenLinks.
html*

Click on links to listen to beluga whales and other ocean animals.

Species at Risk
*http://www.speciesatrisk.
gc.ca/search/default_e.cfm*

Maintained by the Canadian Wildlife Service, this site gives detailed information on different populations of belugas in Canada.

Zoom Whales, Enchanted Learning
*http://www.enchanted
learning.com/subjects/whales/*

This site contains information on all kinds of whales, as well as pictures and classroom activities.

Important Words

baleen huge filters in a baleen whale's mouth that the animal uses to strain out tiny bits of food from seawater

blowhole a whale's nostril, located on the top of the head

blubber a thick layer of fat under the skin of whales and other large ocean mammals

calf a baby whale

Cetacea a group of mostly ocean mammals, including all whales and dolphins

echolocation the process of finding objects by sending out pulses of sound and listening for their echoes

mammals warm-blooded animals that nurse their young and breathe air

melon a fatty organ in the whale's forehead

pods groups of whales

Index

Meet the Author

Ann O. Squire has a PhD in animal behavior. Before becoming a writer, she spent several years studying African electric fish and the special signals they use to communicate with each other. Dr. Squire is the author of many books about natural science and animals, including *Lemmings*, *Moose*, *Penguins*, *Polar Bears*, and *Puffins*. She lives with her family in Katonah, New York.